When we met, the first thing I noticed about you was...

What first attracted me to you was...

I will never forget our first date because...

I first realised I loved you when...

One thing I really admire about you is...

You make me laugh most when...

The cutest thing about you is...

My favorite trip we've taken together so far was...

Our first kiss was...

My favorite funny memory of us is...

My favorite of your quirks is...

Your sexiest feature is...

Our wildest memory together is...

When I first told my friends about you I said...

The weirdest thing I love about you is...

My favorite thing we do together is...

My favorite part of your body is...

The first thing that impressed me about you was...

My favorite scent of yours is...

The way to my heart is when you...

My favorite date of ours so far was...

The thing you do that turns me on the most is...

My favorite gift I've received from you is...

Our song/songs are:

We could talk all day about...

Our special place is...

I am amazed by your knowledge about...

When we're apart, the thing I miss the most about you is...

I knew you were the one when...

You make me feel most special when you...

You look hottest to me when you wear...

A song that reminds me of you is...

Your sexiest personality trait is...

I love that thing you do when you...

Before I met you I would never...

The most unique thing about you is...

I (secretly) love our debates about...

I knew we were perfect for each other when...

The most romantic thing you've ever done is...

The thing you introduced me to that I now love is...

If there was a movie about our love story I'd call it...

One thing I've never told you I love about you is...

The thing you understand about me that noone else does is...

One thing I secretly fantasize about doing with you is...

I love telling people about your...

If we were a Prince and Princess from a movie we would be...

I'll never let you forget that time when...

The one annoying thing about you I can't help but love you for is...

I'm the only one that knows about your secret love of...

I'm passionate about our shared love of...

You make my heart melt most when you...

If I wrote a poem about our love story I'd call it...

I absolutely love your taste in...

The thing that makes me most proud that you're mine is...

I'm obsessed with your...

My favorite movie we've seen together is...

My top 3 favorite intimate moments with you are...

You could win an award for...

If I had to describe you in 5 words,
they would be...

The thing you don't think I notice about you (but I do) is...

I love that you're always there for me when...

One thing you have made me realise about myself is...

The thing I appreciate most about you is...

You are especially talented at...

You make me happiest when you...

The thing you know about me that noone else does is...

The thing I know about you that noone else does is...

My greatest weakness is when you...

The thing I'm most proud of you for doing is...

You're most charming when you...

The biggest challenge we've got through together is...

I love it when you call me...

My favorite pastime of ours is...

I couldn't live without your...

The best thing we've achieved together is...

The weirdest thing we love to do together is...

We work well together because...

When you're in my arms I feel...

We're unstoppable when we...

I love to watch you...

I'm grateful you're mine because...

If you were a wine you'd be...

The thing you dislike about yourself that I love about you is...

The little things I love about you are...

The one memory of us I will never forget is...

The famous couple we're most like is...

You've made me a better person because...

3 places I want to visit with you in the future are...

3 things I want to experience with you are...

I'd still love you even if you were...

The one thing you've said to me that I'll never forget is...

My favorite holiday we've been on was...

The kindest thing you've done for me is...

I love your sense of humor because...

You're the only one who can make me feel...

The naughtiest thing we've done together is...

The thing I'm looking forward to doing with you most is...

Our three inside jokes are...

Being with you has made me realise....

The single greatest thing about our relationship is...

Made in United States
Troutdale, OR
09/24/2023

13151533R00058